MISSING

SARAH HUTT

ASTONISHING HEADLINES

Attacked	**Missing**
Captured	Shot Down
Condemned	Stowed Away
Kidnapped	Stranded at Sea
Lost and Found	Trapped

Development: Kent Publishing Services, Inc.
Design and Production: Signature Design Group, Inc.

SADDLEBACK EDUCATIONAL PUBLISHING

Website: www.sdlback.com

Photo Credits: page 17, NY Photo Press; page 35, NASA; page 59, Larry Lipsky, Index Stock Imagery

ISBN-13: 978-1-56254-824-7
ISBN-10: 1-56254-824-7
eBook: 978-1-60291-009-6

Printed in the United States of America

15 14 13 12 11   6 7 8 9 10 11

TABLE OF CONTENTS

Introduction

Missing. Lost. Gone without a trace. No clues. Sometimes, only a mystery remains. Have you ever had your favorite CD or shirt go missing? You might get mad or annoyed looking for it. But what happens when a real treasure goes missing, or a space ship, or a person? Missing persons leave behind anxious and terrified loved ones.

Missing criminals are fugitives on the run from the law. They might have been captured by police officers, but then escaped. Or they might be suspects on the run, trying to avoid arrest. For crime fighters, it is very important to find missing criminals and make sure they are not a danger to the public.

It can be very sad, scary, or tragic when something important goes missing. Whole ships have vanished without a trace. Entire species of animals or plants can vanish from Earth. At first glance, it can seem as if there are no clues. But determined detectives and scientists look for answers.

Some of these disappearances have puzzled experts for years. With very few clues, they have to work out what exactly happened. Some of these disappearances are solved through detective work and luck. Others remain mysteries, never to be solved.

The FBI's Ten Most Wanted
DATAFILE

TIMELINE

July 1908

Theodore Roosevelt creates the FBI.

March 1950

FBI creates the "Ten Most Wanted Fugitives" list.

June 1999

Terrorist Osama bin Laden is added to the FBI's Ten Most Wanted list.

Where is Washington, D.C.?

terrorist - a person who tries to attack a country or group using violence

federal - having to do with the U.S. government

database - a computerized list of information

parole - a closely watched prisoner on release from jail

DID YOU KNOW?

Only seven women have made the FBI's Ten Most Wanted list. The first was Ruth Eisemann-Schier. Eisemann-Schier was wanted for kidnapping a Miami heiress in Decatur, Georgia. Eisemann-Schier later demanded $500,000 ransom for her safe return.

Chapter One:
The FBI's Ten Most Wanted

What is the FBI?

FBI stands for Federal Bureau of Investigation. The FBI captures people who break federal laws. Federal laws are those that apply to the country as a whole, not just to a single city or state.

The FBI also finds criminals who cross state lines. If a criminal commits crimes in more than one state, his or her crimes become a national concern. This is when the FBI helps local and state police catch the criminals.

The FBI also protects the United States from international criminals. International criminals are people who live in the United States, but commit crimes in other countries. There are also foreign criminals, such as terrorists, who target the United States.

FBI Beginnings

President Theodore Roosevelt created the FBI in July 1908. In the FBI's early days, there were very few federal crimes. Investigators spent most of their time tracking down stolen goods and solving bank robberies. Capturing high-profile fugitives did not become important for the FBI until the 1950s.

J. Edgar Hoover became the director of the FBI in 1924, when he was only 29 years old. He set out to enlarge the FBI's role as a crime-fighting organization. Hoover introduced new programs, some of which are still used by the FBI today.

In 1926, Hoover started a fingerprint file. Fingerprints are used to help identify criminals. This file turned into one of the largest fingerprint databases in the world.

Toughest Criminals

Hoover's other important idea was the FBI's Ten Most Wanted list. This list is an important crime-fighting tool. It is still used today.

The FBI's Ten Most Wanted Fugitives is a list of the 10 fugitives the FBI wants to catch the most. The list includes the name, a description, and a picture of each criminal. It also tells why the criminal is wanted. The list's purpose is to keep the public on the lookout for criminals on the run.

The idea came about when a reporter named Sam Fogg called the FBI one day in 1949.

Sam worked for the International News Service. He did not have any breaking news to report, so he decided to find out what or whom the FBI was investigating. He asked the FBI for the name and description of the 10 "toughest guys" they were tracking.

Fogg went on to write stories about these men for the news service. As a result, two of the men on the list were caught. Hoover realized the success of this idea and created a permanent list of the Ten Most Wanted Fugitives in March 1950.

The First Catch

The first person on the list was Thomas J. Holden. He was convicted of robbery and sent to prison. After many years in jail, he was released on parole. While Holden was free, he shot and killed his wife and her two brothers. Then he went on the run.

The FBI put his picture on the list. Back then, the Ten Most Wanted list was posted in post offices, general stores, and newspapers.

In June 1951, an Oregon resident spotted Holden. He was working under a different name. The resident told the FBI and Holden was captured.

Since that time, 478 fugitives have appeared on the list. Of that number, 448 have been found and arrested.

Today's Ten Most Wanted

In the 1950s, most of the criminals on the list were bank robbers, car thieves, and murderers. As the times changed, so did the types of criminals on the list.

Over the last 54 years, the list has included gangsters, drug dealers, and terrorists. Criminals are put on the list because they have a history of committing serious crimes, or they are very dangerous. Criminals are removed from the list only if they are captured or no longer considered dangerous. When a fugitive is taken off the list, the FBI adds a new one. The FBI only lists criminals they think will be caught by showing them to the public. High-profile criminals in the news usually do not make the list.

However, one of the most recent additions to the list has received a lot of attention in the news. In June 1999, international terrorist, Osama bin Laden (also spelled Usama) was added to the list. He is accused of causing the death of American citizens by organizing many terrorist attacks.

America's Most Wanted

In July 1981, John Walsh's six-year-old son, Adam, was abducted and killed. John Walsh and his wife were very sad about their son's death. They decided to try and stop criminals from hurting other people. They started the television program *America's Most Wanted* in 1987.

The show broadcasts pictures and information about America's most wanted criminals. TV viewers can call in and report criminals if they spot them on the street. So far, the show has helped capture nearly 800 fugitives!

Famous Cases, Funny Names

Bank robberies and police shootouts with gangsters were the crimes of the 1920s to 1950s. Here are some famous FBI cases.

"Baby Face" Nelson

"Baby Face" Nelson was called "Baby Face" due to his young appearance. Nelson was wanted for the murder of five FBI agents, armed robbery, and auto theft in a crime spree from1922–1934.

Charles A. "Pretty Boy" Floyd

"Pretty Boy" Floyd was wanted for his part in The Kansas City Massacre in 1933, in which five men died. Floyd was a bank robber and a murderer.

George "Machine Gun" Kelley

"Machine Gun" Kelley was wanted by the FBI for kidnapping wealthy businessman, Charles F. Urschel in1933.

OSAMA BIN LADEN

Aliases: Usama bin Muhammad bin Ladin, Shaykh Usama bin Ladin, the Prince, the Emir, Abu Abdallah, Mujahid Shaykh, Hajj, the Director

Date of Birth: 1957
Hair: Brown
Place of Birth: Saudi Arabia
Eyes: Brown
Height: 6' 4" to 6' 6"
Complexion: Olive
Weight: 160 pounds
Sex: Male
Build: Thin
Nationality: Saudi Arabian
Occupation: Unknown
Scars and Marks: None
Bin Laden is the leader of the terrorist group Al-Qaeda, "The Base." He is left handed and walks with a cane.

FBI TEN MOST WANTED FUGITIVE

MURDER OF U.S. NATIONALS OUTSIDE THE UNITED STATES;
CONSPIRACY TO MURDER U.S. NATIONALS OUTSIDE THE UNITED STATES;
ATTACK ON A FEDERAL FACILITY RESULTING IN DEATH

USAMA BIN LADEN

Date of Photograph Unknown

Aliases: Usama Bin Muhammad Bin Ladin, Shaykh Usama Bin Ladin, the Prince, the Emir, Abu Abdallah, Mujahid Shaykh, Hajj, the Director

DESCRIPTION

Date of Birth:	1957	**Hair:**	Brown
Place of Birth:	Saudi Arabia	**Eyes:**	Brown
Height:	6' 4" to 6' 6"	**Complexion:**	Olive
Weight:	Approximately 160 pounds	**Sex:**	Male
Build:	Thin	**Nationality:**	Saudi Arabian
Occupation(s):	Unknown		
Remarks:	He is the leader of a terrorist organization known as Al-Qaeda "The Base." He walks with a cane.		

CAUTION

USAMA BIN LADEN IS WANTED IN CONNECTION WITH THE AUGUST 7, 1998, BOMBINGS OF
THE UNITED STATES EMBASSIES IN DAR ES SALAAM, TANZANIA AND NAIROBI, KENYA.
THESE ATTACKS KILLED OVER 200 PEOPLE.

CONSIDERED ARMED AND EXTREMELY DANGEROUS

IF YOU HAVE ANY INFORMATION CONCERNING THIS PERSON, PLEASE CONTACT YOUR
LOCAL FBI OFFICE OR THE NEAREST U.S. EMBASSY OR CONSULATE.

REWARD

The United States Government is offering a reward of up to $5 million for information leading directly
to the apprehension or conviction of Usama Bin Laden.

www.fbi.gov

Osama bin Laden's wanted poster

The Bermuda Triangle
DATAFILE

TIMELINE

December 1944
Flight 19 disappears over the Bermuda Triangle.

February 1960
Journalist Vincent H. Gaddis makes up the name "Bermuda Triangle."

Where is the Bermuda Triangle?

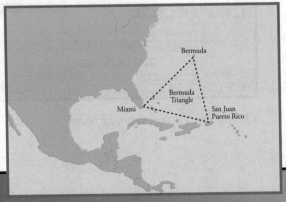

KEY TERMS

compass - a magnetic tool that points to the direction you are heading

true north - the direction of the North Pole

supernatural - beyond natural or scientific forces

phenomenon - an amazing or hard to explain event

portal - a door or entrance; a way in or out

magnetic north - the northerly direction of Earth's magnetic north pole

vessels - boats, ships

DID YOU KNOW?

The "Devil's Sea" is the only place other than the Bermuda Triangle where compasses point to true north. The "Devil's Sea" is off Japan's east coast.

Chapter Two:
The Bermuda Triangle

The Bermuda Triangle is an area of the Atlantic Ocean covered in mystery. Also called "The Devil's Triangle," this spot has been the site of many disappearances. Since the 1900s, more than 50 ships and 20 planes have gone missing in the Bermuda Triangle. Many of these boats and planes just vanished. They made no distress calls and left no wreckage behind.

The Bermuda triangle is a stretch of water that forms a triangle between eastern Florida, the islands of Bermuda, and Puerto Rico. The triangle is more than 500,000 square miles in size. For some, crossing the triangle can be a scary experience because of the mystery that surrounds it.

Over time, the mystery of the missing ships and planes led many people to believe supernatural forces were at work in the triangle.

Flight 19

One of the most famous Bermuda Triangle mysteries is the disappearance of Flight 19. Flight 19 was a squadron of five Avenger torpedo bombers. On December 5, 1944, the planes left the Fort Lauderdale Florida Naval Air Station at 2:00 P.M. It was a training mission with a team of 13 students and one commander.

At around 3:00 P.M., the commander radioed to say his compass had stopped working. He believed he was close to Florida. But actually, the team was really headed in a different direction. They continued to fly further out into the ocean.

By nightfall, the team did not know where they were and had also lost radio contact. The weather was getting bad and the planes were low on fuel.

Three other planes were sent out to look for Flight 19. Among them was a Martin Mariner. By the next morning, not only was Flight 19 missing, but the Martin Mariner had disappeared as well.

What Happened to Flight 19?

Historians believe that Flight 19's crew simply got lost. The commander did not realize the difference in his compass readings in the Bermuda Triangle. He steered the planes out into the ocean until they were lost. They got too far out to communicate by radio.

Experts believe the planes ran out of fuel, and then crashed into the ocean.

The heavy iron planes instantly sank to the ocean floor and were swept away.

Many people believe the Martin Mariner airplane that searched for Flight 19 blew up. These planes were known to leak fuel when they were flying. Sailors at sea saw an explosion right after the Mariner took off from Banana River Naval Air Station.

It is very likely that one of the passengers on the plane lit a cigarette. The plane, full of fumes, instantly blew up. It sank and was never found.

Supernatural Stories

Over the years, many other ships and planes have sailed or flown off into the Bermuda Triangle, never to be seen again. All kinds of spectacular stories try to explain the Bermuda Triangle's phenomenon.

These stories include a giant octopus that attacks planes and sinks ships. Another idea is that aliens built a portal to another dimension in the triangle. This portal supposedly opens 25 times a year and transports ships and planes to another world where they stay trapped in space and time.

However, scientists and experts have worked hard to explain away these legends. Scientists believe there are scientific reasons why so many ships and planes go down in this area.

What's in a Name?

The "Bermuda Triangle," is not recognized as an official name for this mysterious stretch of ocean. A journalist named Vincent H. Gaddis made up the name for an article in the magazine "Argosy" in February 1964.

The article was about the strange number of disappearances in the area.

Gaddis's article got people interested in the Bermuda Triangle's mysteries. It also helped spread the spooky legends surrounding the Bermuda Triangle.

The Real Story

The Bermuda Triangle is one of two places in the world where compasses point to the North Pole, or true north. Usually compasses point to magnetic north. Navigators adjust their steering because of the difference in true north and magnetic north. But if they do this in the Bermuda Triangle, they will head in the wrong direction and get lost.

The Bermuda Triangle is also known for quick changes in weather. Warm tropical air from the islands constantly bumps into colder air from the United

States. This causes flash storms, waterspouts, and dangerous traveling conditions.

Finally, sailor and pilot error is always a possibility. Accidents can happen without warning. The Bermuda Triangle is a busy part of the ocean. Because there are many ships in this area, there are bound to be many accidents. The Bermuda Triangle's strong currents also sweep shipwrecks away into deep holes in the ocean floor. When ships sink in the Bermuda Triangle, they truly are gone without a trace.

Scientists and historians challenge themselves to solve supernatural events with logical explanations. If the wrecks are found, they will have evidence to prove their theories. As long as these vessels remain missing, we can never really know what happened.

Disappearances

These are just some of the ships and planes believed to be lost in the Bermuda Triangle in the last 10 years.

1994, December 25: plane missing over Florida; pilot lost.

1995, March 20: boat: *Jamanic K.* missing on route from Haiti to Miami.

1996, May 2: Atlantic/Caribbean charter plane missing with 3 aboard.

1996, October 14: boat: *Intrepid* missing 30 miles off Fort Pierce, FL; 16 aboard.

1997, December: boat: *Robalo* missing off Virginia Beach.

1998, January 2: boat: *Grumpy* found derelict.

1998, May 1: boat: *Miss Charlotte* hit by a force that sucked everything off deck, then sunk; crew survived. Thought to be a water spout; off North Carolina coast.

1998, August 10: boat: *Erica Lynn* missing.

1998, August 19: Atlantic/Caribbean charter plane missing; 4 aboard.

1998, November: boat: *Carolina* missing off Cape May coast.

1998, November: boat: *Interlude* disappeared during cruise to Cayman Islands.

1999, April 15: boat: *Miss Fernandina* missing off Flagler Beach, FL.; last signaled: net caught in propeller, electrical drain, listing.

1999, April 23: boat: *Genesis* sailed from Port of Spain.

1999, May 12, plane missing near Nassau, Bahamas; pilot aboard.

1999, August 5: boat: Unknown name found derelict except for the dog; off North Carolina coast.

1999, November 15: boat: Unknown name missing between Frying Pan Shoals and Frying Pan Light, North Carolina; 2 aboard.

1999, December 27, boat: *Alyson Selene* found derelict 7 miles northeast of Andros, Bahamas.

2000, April, freighter: *Gran Rio R* disappears off West Indies coast.

2000, August 14, boat: *Hemmingway* is found deserted; missing crew and captain.

2001, June 22, boat: *Tropic Bird* is found derelict off Antigua.

2001, October 27, plane missing after leaving Winterhaven, FL; pilot aboard.

2002, September 23, freighter: *Fiona R* missing off West Indies en route to St. Vincent.

2002, November 25, boat: *Peanuts Too* is found deserted south of Bermuda.

2003, September 6, plane missing southeast of Nassau, Bahamas; pilot aboard.

Mission to Mars

DATAFILE

TIMELINE

July and September 1976

Viking 1 and *Viking 2* land on Mars.

July 1988

Phobos I and *Phobos II* travel to Mars.

July 1997

Pathfinder lands on Mars.

Where is Mars?

orbit - to move about something in a circular path

telescope - an instrument for viewing distant objects by refracting light rays through a lens or the reflection of light rays by a concave mirror

astronomer - a scientist who studies Earth, planets, stars, and space

NASA - National Aeronautics and Space Administration: the team that runs the U.S. space program

DID YOU KNOW?

Mars has two moons orbiting the planet. They are called Phobos and Deimos. *Phobos* is Greek for "fear." *Deimos* is Greek for "panic."

Chapter Three:
Mission to Mars

The planet Mars is Earth's closest neighbor. Mars is also called the Red Planet. Early stargazers noticed the color and thought it looked like blood. Because of this they named the planet after Mars, the Roman god of war. Its red color is due to rusting metal particles on the planet's surface.

With the invention of the telescope, early astronomers got a better look at Mars. In the late 1800s, an astronomer named Percival Lowell thought he could see canals on Mars' surface. Lowell believed that intelligent life forms must have built them.

As telescopes improved, astronomers saw that there were no canals on Mars.

However, the idea that Martians might live on the planet interested scientists and thrilled people.

Today, scientists have made great progress in trying to answer the question: "Is there life on Mars?"

Lost in Space

Since the 1960s, there have been 37 missions to Mars. Many different countries have launched these missions. But only spacecraft 17 made it to Mars and were able to send information to Earth.

The earliest missions were flybys of the planet. These spacecraft took pictures of the planet and beamed them back to Earth. Later spacecraft orbited Mars. These orbit missions meant the spacecraft spent more time close to Mars. They sent back better pictures.

A Martian Mystery

In the summer of 1976, *Viking 1* and *2* were the first spacecraft to land on Mars. Their successful landing began a new era of Mars exploration.

Viking 1 and *2* could not move once they reached Mars' surface. However, they did take a picture that made many people wonder about life on Mars.

In one photo there appeared to be a human face. NASA scientists decided it was a natural rock formation that just happened to look like a face. But more eerie pictures were soon taken of Mars.

The first photograph ever taken from the surface of Mars by the Viking I *lander, 1976.*

Sojourner Success Story

On July 4, 1997, a U.S. spacecraft called the *Pathfinder* landed on Mars. It opened its doors and released a small robot car or rover, called *Sojourner*.

Sojourner's mission was to roam the Martian surface and study rocks and dirt. Scientists believed that clues about life on Mars could be found in the rocks on the planet's surface.

When *Sojourner* finally made it to Mars, it did not send back any alien pictures. But it did send back the first in-depth information about the Martian surface.

NASA scientists controlled *Sojourner* by radio signals beamed from Earth. Every signal took 11 minutes to travel 93 million miles to Mars.

From the rocks *Sojourner* collected, scientists discovered that there was once water on the dry planet. On Earth, where there is water, there is life. This discovery of water traces on Mars helped prove that there might have been life on Mars some time in the past.

Martian Mystery

In July 1988, the USSR sent two landers called *Phobos* I and *Phobos* II to study Phobos. Phobos is one of the two moons that orbit Mars.

Phobos I shut down on its way to Mars. It was powered by solar panels. At some point, *Phobos* I got lost and pointed its panels away from the sun. The panels could not charge and it quickly lost power.

Phobos II seemed to do better. It stayed in contact with Earth until right before it was about to drop to the moon's surface. Then communications were lost. It is not known if *Phobos II* made it to Phobos' surface.

The last pictures *Phobos II* beamed back to Earth were amazing. There appeared to be a long dark object on the surface of Mars!

News reporters told the world of the strange images. Many people wondered if these images were alien buildings on Mars. People wondered if aliens could have shut down *Phobos I* and *II*.

Soviet scientists said that the image was actually the shadow of the moon, Phobos, on the Martian surface. Because Phobos is not perfectly round, and the surface of Mars is not flat, the shadow made a strange shape. Still, many UFO followers did not believe this explanation.

Mars Observer is Missing

When the U.S. lander *Mars Observer* suddenly lost communications, scientists were puzzled. On August 22, 1993, the spacecraft prepared to orbit Mars. Without warning, its transmitters turned off. Scientists believe that there was a leak in the ship's steering systems and it lost control.

Since *Sojourner's* success, there have been several more missions to Mars. Some have run into problems. Some, like the *Mars Odyssey* and *the Mars Global Surveyor* are successfully orbiting the planet. In January 2004, twin rovers *Spirit* and *Opportunity* roam across the Martian surface. The search for life on Mars continues.

Missions to Mars

There have been many missions to Mars in the last 40 years. Here are some of them. There are many more planned for the future.

Marsnik 1and 2 - October 1960 USSR
  Attempted Mars Flyby
  (Launch Failure)

Sputnik 22 - October 1962 USSR
  Attempted Mars Flyby

Mars 1 - November 1962 USSR
  Mars Flyby (Contact Lost)

Sputnik 24 - November 1962 USSR
  Attempted Mars Lander

Mariner 3 and 4 - November 1964 USA
  Mars Flyby

Zond 2 - November 1964 USSR
  Mars Flyby (Contact Lost)

Mariner 6 and 7 - Summer 1969 USA
  Mars Flyby

Mars 1969A and B - Spring 1969 USSR
  Attempted Mars Orbiter
  (Launch Failure)

Mariner 8 - May 1971 USA
  Attempted Mars Flyby (Launch Failure)

Kosmos 419 - May 1971 USSR
 Attempted Mars Orbiter/Lander

Mars 2 and 3 - May 1971 USSR
  Mars Orbiter/Attempted Lander

Mariner 9 - May 1971 USA
  Mars Orbiter

Mars 4, 5, 6, and 7 - Summer 1973 USSR
  Mars Flyby, Orbiter, and Lander

Viking 1 and 2 - Summer 1975 USA
  Mars Orbiter/Lander

Phobos I and II - July 1988 USSR
  Attempted Mars Orbiter/Phobos Landers

Mars Observer - September 1992 USA
  Attempted Mars Orbiter (Contact Lost)

Mars Global Surveyor - November 1996
  USA Mars Orbiter

Mars 96 - November 1996 Russia
  Attempted Mars Orbiter/Lander

Mars Pathfinder - December 1996 USA
  Mars Lander/Rover

Nozomi (Planet-B) - July 1998 Japan
  Mars Orbiter

Mars Climate Orbiter - December 1998
USA Attempted Mars Orbiter

Mars Polar Lander and Deep Space 2 -
January 1999 USA Attempted Mars Lander

Mars Odyssey - April 2001 USA
  Mars Orbiter

Mars Express - June 2003 USA
  Mars Orbiter/Lander

Spirit and Opportunity - Summer 2003
USA Mars Rovers

Mars Reconnaissance Orbiter - August
  2005 USA Mars Orbiter

Phoenix - Late 2007 USA
  Small Mars Scout Lander

Netlanders - Late 2007 France
  Mars Netlanders

Mars 2009 - Late 2009 USA
  Mars Science Laboratory Rover

Mars 2011 - 2011 USA
  Scout Mission

Missing Treasure Found

DATAFILE

1681

The *Santa Maria De La Consolación* leaves Peru filled with Inca treasure. It soon sinks.

1990s

Two brothers in Ecuador find *Santa Maria's* lost treasure while walking on the beach.

Where is Santa Clara, Ecuador?

galleon - a Spanish sailing ship

Incas - an ancient group of people who lived in South America from 1200 to the 1500s

Viceroy of Peru - the Spanish governor of the land captured by the conquistadors

salvage - to rescue a ship, its crew, or cargo from a shipwreck

DID YOU KNOW?

In South America, the Spanish conquerors, such as Pizarro, Cortes, Orellana, and Cabeza de Vaca, were called *conquistadors*.

Chapter Four:
Missing Treasure Found

In 1681, a Spanish galleon called the *Santa Maria De La Consolación* left Peru filled with Inca treasure. The ship traveled up the coast of South America to Panama. Captain Juan de Lerma had heard that pirates prowled the waters on the way to Panama. He wanted to delay his trip so he might avoid them. But the Viceroy of Peru ordered the ship to set sail. The treasure had to be in Panama before the Spanish fleet left for Spain. De Lerma followed his orders and set sail for Panama.

Off of the coast of Ecuador, a pirate ship under the command of Captain Sharpe attacked the *Santa Maria*. The attack was so bloody that to this day Ecuadorians call the nearby island of

Santa Clara "El Muerto." This means "the dead."

The *Santa Maria*'s crew fought the pirates until the ship ran into a reef. Trapped, de Lerma ordered his men to burn the ship and protect the treasure. The ship went down full of treasure.

Captain Sharpe was so mad that he killed every man from the *Santa Maria* —350 in all. The shark infested waters made it impossible for Sharpe's men to get the treasure. It remained lost in its watery grave, forgotten.

Forgotten Fortune

In the 1990s, two brothers went for a walk along the beach of Santa Clara Island. One of them noticed a black stone rolling in the surf. He picked it up to look closer. He quickly realized that it was not a stone. It was a 300-year-old Spanish coin!

Word of the coin spread quickly. Roberto Aguirre, a wealthy businessman, set out to investigate which ship the coin had come from.

But the treasure hunt did not start in the ocean, it started in a library. Aguirre hired a professional treasure hunter named Joel Ruth. Ruth was an expert in coins and began searching for records of ships carrying this kind of coin. He found the *Santa Maria* story. From there he traced her location.

Scouring the Seas

For six years, Aguirre, Ruth, and a team of divers searched the ocean around Santa Clara. Divers found a trail of coins that stretched for miles on the ocean floor. The coins had been swept away from the ship by the current.

But as the divers got closer, they still could not find the wreck. Then one day, a local fisherman called for help. The fisherman told the divers that his net was caught on something in 30 feet of water. They went down to investigate and could not believe their eyes. Below them, under sand and seaweed, were large wooden beams. The beams were blackened from fire.

The divers collected samples of the wood to be tested. The tests showed that the wood was at least 370 years old. This was the same age as the *Santa Maria De La Consolación*.

Missing Treasure Lost Again?

The treasure aboard the *Santa Maria* was thought to be worth between $20 to $100 million dollars.

As far as the divers could tell, this wreck had never been discovered. This meant that all the treasure should still be on or near the ship.

The team of divers wanted to return to the wreck quickly. But when they returned, the wreck was gone. The ocean currents had covered the wood beams. The *Santa Maria* was once again hidden.

However, this time they knew where to look. The divers brought in high-powered water cannons to blow away the sand. Once again they uncovered the wreck. With the permission of the Ecuadorian government, the team began to salvage the wreck. They recovered coins, pottery, jewels, and gold. Most of all, they recovered the missing *Santa Maria De La Consolación*.

Spanish Treasure Fleets

After Columbus made his famous voyage to the new world in 1492, Spain became Europe's most powerful country. The Spanish navy was unbeatable for almost 100 years.

Spain established trade routes from conquered lands in Central and South America back to Spain. The Spanish ships brought goods from Europe to colonial settlers. They then brought back treasures from the New World.

These ships were known as treasure fleets, or *flotas* in Spanish. There were two main fleets, the *Tierra Firme* and the *Nueva España*. Each fleet was made up of many ships. The merchant ships carried the treasure. Smaller ships scouted for pirates. And large, heavily armed gun ships protected them all.

Spanish Conquistadors and the End of the Inca Empire

The Incas were an ancient people who ruled a large empire in South America. They ruled from their capital, which today is the city of Cuzco in Peru.

The Incas were religious. They worshiped the natural world, sun, and moon. They were great astronomers, and they built great cities and temples. They ruled their empire from 1200 to 1532, when the Spanish conquered their empire.

The Spanish explorer Pizarro came to the Inca rulers and asked them to become Christians. The Inca emperor, Atahuallpa, refused and was captured by the Spanish and killed. This began the destruction of the Inca Empire. Spain claimed the Inca's gold and silver treasures and sent them back to Spain.

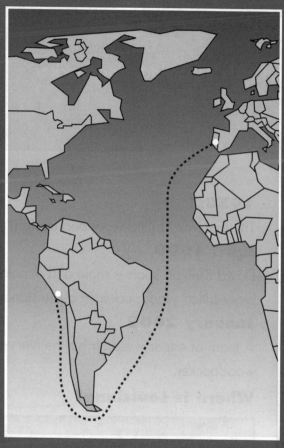

The Spanish conquistadors shipped the treasures they seized from South America back to Spain.

The Ivory-billed Woodpecker
DATAFILE

TIMELINE

1950s
The last ivory-billed woodpecker sighting.

April 1999
David Kulivan spots a male and female ivory-billed woodpecker in a Louisiana forest.

January 2002
A team of experts search for the ivory-billed woodpecker.

Where is Louisiana?

unique - one-of-a-kind or original

habitat - the special kind of area where a plant or an animal lives

forestry - the study of caring for forests and forest wildlife

skeptic - a person who doubts something until he or she sees proof

Woodpeckers have *zygodactyl* feet. This means they have two toes pointing forward and two pointing backwards. These toes help them climb trees.

Chapter Five:
The Ivory-billed Woodpecker

The ivory-billed woodpecker is native to the southeast United States. That is, it lived there until the 1950s. At that time, bird watchers no longer spotted these unique birds.

The male ivory-billed woodpecker has a bright red crest on its head. The males and females both have long white bills. They use their bills to tear bark from dead trees. They then eat insect larva growing under the bark.

The ivory-billed woodpecker is America's largest woodpecker. The birds are 20 inches tall. Their wings are three feet from tip to tip. Their calls sound like a toy trumpet.

When years passed without any sightings of the ivory-billed woodpeckers, bird watchers believed they were extinct. Bird watchers believed hunting and logging of the bird's habitat had wiped out the bird. But in 1999, many bird watchers changed their minds.

A Walk in the Woods

In 1999, David Kulivan was a forestry student at Louisiana State University. On April Fool's Day, he decided to go turkey hunting. He set out for the Pearl River Wildlife Management Area near New Orleans. This forest covers 35,000 acres. It is filled with old trees and swamps.

As Kulivan walked through the forest, he spotted a pair of ivory-billed woodpeckers—a male and a female. His sighting was the first time anyone got a good look at the birds in nearly 50 years!

When Kulivan reported his sighting, many people did not believe him. But he gave a good description of the male's red crest, their white bills, and their unique call. Soon, the skeptics were convinced his sighting was real.

A Search Gets Started

In January 2002, three years after Kulivan's sighting, a search for the birds started. A German company called Zeiss paid for a research trip into the Pearl River Wildlife Management Area. The company organized a team of six top bird watchers from around the world.

The Zeiss team spent a month hiking through the forest and swamps looking for the birds. They looked up into the dead trees where the birds usually fed. They also looked for areas where they might nest. The used high-tech digital cameras and sound equipment to try to find the birds.

After searching for a month, the Zeiss team was not able to find the birds. But they did find signs of the ivory-billed woodpecker. They found possible nests and feeding areas.

Do They Exist?

Even though the Zeiss team did not find the birds, many people remain hopeful that the birds will be found. Bird watchers are thrilled at the idea that the ivory-billed woodpecker might exist. The ivory-billed woodpecker is a majestic bird. Many people think it is a symbol of America's natural beauty.

Woodpecker Stats

- The ivory-billed woodpecker is the largest woodpecker in North America.

- Ivory-billed woodpeckers can be from 19–21 inches in length.

- Ivory-billed woodpeckers build their nests in trees.

- Female ivory-billed woodpeckers usually lay up to three eggs at a time.

- Ivory-billed woodpeckers eat insect larvae that grow in hollow trees.

- Ivory-billed woodpeckers are solitary birds, and do not live in a flock.

- Ivory-billed woodpeckers do not spend much time in one place. They roam over large feeding territories.

The pileated woodpecker is a close relative of the ivory-billed woodpecker.

Book Review

Guiberson, Brenda Z., *Tales of the Haunted Deep*. New York: Holt and Company, 2000.

Mysterious and spooky stories about the sea fill the gripping book *Tales of the Haunted Deep*. For even more suspense, the book is divided into five themes:

- Chills from the Sea
- The Dreaded Pirate Ghost
- Swish, Swirl, Sea Serpent!
- The Lighthouse Ghosts
- Ghostly Ships with a Mind of Their Own

Each section contains several different creepy and ghostly stories and memorable mysteries.

One story describes the ghost of Blackbeard the pirate searching for his missing head. Legend has it Blackbeard was killed by British sailors in a vicious battle with the British navy. The sailors cut off the pirate's head and hung it from the ship. Since then, his headless ghost has haunted the seas.

Another story tells the spooky tale of a girl who is missing in a lighthouse. The story begins with a girl and her friends exploring a lighthouse. The girl comes upon a secret door. The door opens to a bottomless pit. Later, the girl returns to the lighthouse, alone. She vanishes, leaving only her bloody handkerchief in front of the door.

The last section in the book includes photos and captions that let you be creative and make up your own stories. Even if you do not believe in the supernatural, this book will keep you reading. By the end of each story, you will hope that sea monsters and ghosts do not really exist.

Glossary

astronomer: a scientist who studies Earth, planets, stars, and space

compass: a magnetic tool that points to the direction you are heading

database: a computerized list of information

federal: having to do with the U.S. government

forestry: the study of caring for forests and forest wildlife

galleon: a Spanish sailing ship

habitat: the special kind of area where a plant or animal lives

Incas: an ancient group of people who lived in South America from 1200 to the 1500s

magnetic north: the direction of Earth's magnetic north pole

NASA: National Aeronautics and Space Administration: the team that runs the U.S. space program

orbit: to move about something in a circular path

parole: a closely watched prisoner on release from jail

phenomenon: an amazing or hard to explain event

portal: a door or entrance; a way in or out

salvage: to rescue a ship, its crew, or cargo from a shipwreck

skeptic: a person who doubts something until he or she sees proof

supernatural: beyond natural or scientific forces

telescope: an instrument for viewing distant objects by refracting light rays through a lens or the reflection of light rays by a concave mirror

terrorist: a person who tries to attack a country or group using violence

true north: the direction of the North Pole

unique: one-of-a-kind or original

vessels: boats, ships

Viceroy of Peru: the Spanish governor of the land captured by the conquistadors

Index